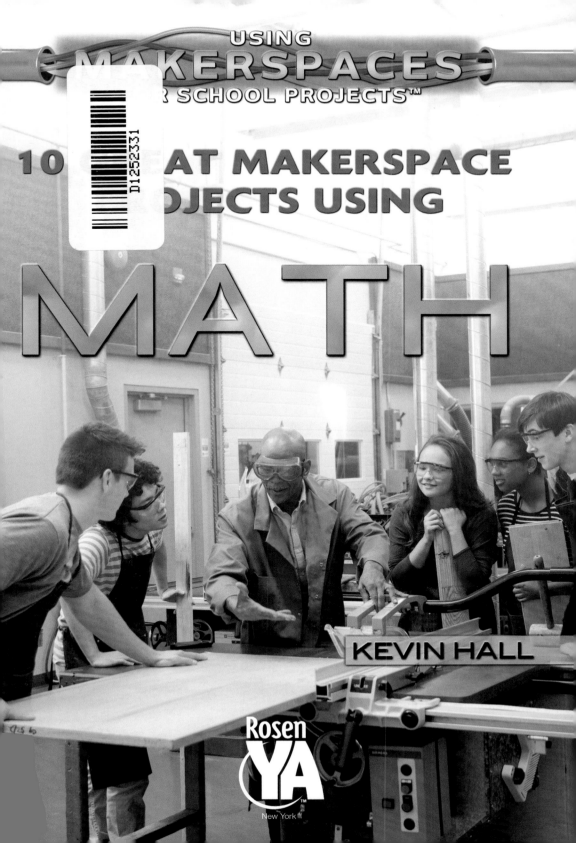

USING
MAKERSPACES
R SCHOOL PROJECTS™

10   AT MAKERSPACE
OJECTS USING

MATH

KEVIN HALL

Rosen
YA™
New York

Published in 2018 by The Rosen Publishing Group, Inc.
29 East 21st Street, New York, NY 10010

Copyright © 2018 by The Rosen Publishing Group, Inc.

First Edition

Library of Congress Cataloging-in-Publication Data

Names: Hall, Kevin, 1990– author.
Title: 10 great makerspace projects using math / Kevin Hall.
Description: First edition. | New York, NY : Rosen Publishing, 2018. | Series: Using makerspaces for school projects | Audience: Grades 6 to 12. | Includes bibliographical references and index.
Identifiers: LCCN 2016056487 | ISBN 9781499438468 (library bound)
Subjects: LCSH: Mathematics—Study and teaching. | Makerspaces—Juvenile literature. | Science projects—Juvenile literature.
Classification: LCC TS171.57 .H35 2018 | DDC 510.78—dc23
LC record available at https://lccn.loc.gov/2016056487

Manufactured in the United States of America

CONTENTS

Makerspaces allow you to create fun, interactive projects that use a wide range of tools. They can be used for any subject and stress creativity and teamwork.

Educators have always used special tools and projects in the classroom. In our society today, technology has made it easier for teachers to have projects in the classroom that help their students develop and learn. One of these developments is the idea of makerspaces. Makerspaces, also known to some as hackspaces or hackerspaces, have become extremely useful tools in the classroom.

Makerspace projects are totally up to the teachers, students, and schools. They are creative, hands-on activities that allow you to collaborate with others to invent, develop, and learn about a specific topic. Given this definition, it is interesting to see how makerspaces are developed in the classroom.

The focus of a makerspace project is up to the educator and student. Whether you use robots, programming, or some other form of electronics, it is important to look back on the definition of a makerspace. It is a community tool used for educational reasons. Here you will find ten projects that students can use in order to learn about various math concepts. There's a whole world of makerspaces out there.

Makerspace projects also produce far-ranging effects *outside* of the classroom. It is true that the makerspace projects are used to educate students about a new topic. This may involve the use of simple tools or advanced ones such as 3D printers and lasers. Whatever the nature of the tools, it is important to note that you also have the chance to learn new social skills. Working together in a makerspace environment helps young people try out new aspects of social interaction as well.

Makerspace projects allow you to take risks and experiment using your own ideas. They allow you to realize that your ideas are valid in your own learning. The hands-on or do-it-yourself approach to learning allows readers to realize that their opinions and questions *actually matter*. The projects listed are meant to both teach and inspire students and educators alike.

Each of these projects includes some form of math concept. From basic math to more advanced concepts, you'll be able to dive into creating, learning, and experimenting all at once. Makerspace math projects are not just fun but also educational. They serve a dual purpose in the classroom, allowing students to both engage in learning and fun, useful activities.

Makerspace projects stress the idea that learning can be an enriching experience inside the classroom. They allow participants to collaborate while flexing their creative muscles. Math concepts remain central to each project. Those who tackle math makerspaces will find themselves challenged to explore new ideas while working with new materials and technology.

CHAPTER ONE

THE MAKER MOVEMENT

Makerspaces have popped up in schools, libraries, and community centers all across the country. These spaces offer interactive and engaging tools to let you create as you learn. In fact, makerspaces have become so popular today that there is a new term for the craze around them: the maker movement.

Makerspaces, and the maker movement in general, have totally changed classroom projects. The goal of makerspaces and the maker movement is to allow you more freedom in your learning. Makerspaces aren't going to totally replace textbooks, outlines, and book reports. They are, however, an unusual approach toward learning in the classroom. Still, makerspaces are much more than classrooms. There are many ways in which makerspaces have a positive effect on the students who engage with them.

For one, makerspace projects offer a new approach to learning. Instead of absorbing facts and figures, makerspaces allow students to instead experiment with new materials and ideas. Makerspace projects value curiosity. They give you a resource to experiment as well as learn in the classroom.

Each member of a team involved in a makerspace project has a certain responsibility to help the team learn and finish the project.

These projects also stress the idea of teamwork. Many of these projects require participants to form groups and work together in order to accomplish the goal. This has long-term effects both inside and out of the classroom. The teamwork idea that all makerspace projects stress helps participants learn the value of working together in groups. It also makes clear the fact that everyone in a group must contribute in order to get a specific task done.

MAKER CULTURE

The so-called maker culture that has come about from the maker movement extends far beyond the classroom. The do-it-yourself attitude has reached into other jobs as well. Whether it's a clothing designer sewing his or her own fabric to create new fashions, a musician creating a new band or sound using homemade instruments, or scientists inventing their own devices with original homemade designs, the maker movement has seen a fair share of development outside of the classroom. Maker Faires are events where creative minds can meet to showcase and discuss their own projects. While makerspace projects are great classroom tools, they also have an impact outside of the classroom.

The making of all these makerspace projects also gives a sense of power to the students themselves. A completed makerspace project is a unique way for a student to prove that he or she has learned something. Rather than doing well on a test or an assignment, a finished makerspace is a direct way of a student showing he or she has mastered a certain concept. The maker

(continued on the next page)

Maker Faires have become a worldwide phenomenon and provide makers the opportunity to discuss what they have built and what they've learned.

(*continued from the previous page*)

movement has inspired students and teachers to be excited about learning.

Makerspaces also allow you to experi-ment *and fail*. In makerspaces, teachers can encourage you to apply your knowledge and make mistakes. Instead of punishing participants for making mistakes in their makerspace project, teachers instead can encourage them to regroup and think of new ways to make their makerspace project the best it can possibly be. There are no failures in makerspace projects. There are only ways you can learn to fix your mistakes.

There is a clear, three-step process involved in every makerspace project. The first involves the student being presented with a challenge. This challenge will be solved by creating the project itself. This part of the process involves many skills young people already know: brainstorming, researching, calculating, and so on.

Students learn how to use certain tools to complete their makerspace projects, a hands-on approach enhances learning.

The second part of the process involves actually making at the makerspace. Using the information the makers have come up with after being presented with the challenge, this is the main part of the makerspace process. This "making" demonstrates your knowledge. It's a direct way of displaying the knowledge you've put forth.

The last step is analyzing the finished project. Students and teachers can come together and see what went right with their projects. They can also see what can be improved or changed the next time the makerspace project is performed. The students can see whether their original plans were followed and what they can do to make their projects even better.

Makerspace projects serve as innovative ways to introduce specific topics and allow you to prove that you have learned about the topic. There are countless makerspace projects that any class can do, regardless of subject. Makerspaces are very useful when dealing with math concepts. Whether it's simple algebra or more complicated topics like programming and coding, makerspaces can be used to enhance math lessons.

CHAPTER TWO

BASIC PROJECTS (PART 1)

Makerspace projects are interesting in that the project can be as simple or complex as you want it to be. Many makerspace math projects use technology such as 3D printers and laser cutters. But there are also many that don't require anything that advanced. When dealing with basic math concepts, you can use simple techniques and strategies in makerspace projects.

Simple equations are a concept that can be taught using makerspaces. Instead of using some form of laser or a 3D printer, however, this makerspace project uses much simpler materials but is still useful in helping you create and learn at the same time.

PROJECT 1: MATH SCRABBLE

Math Scrabble (also known as Number Scrabble) is a makerspace project that can be used to demonstrate simple equations. The materials you need are a game board, tiles, and a permanent marker.

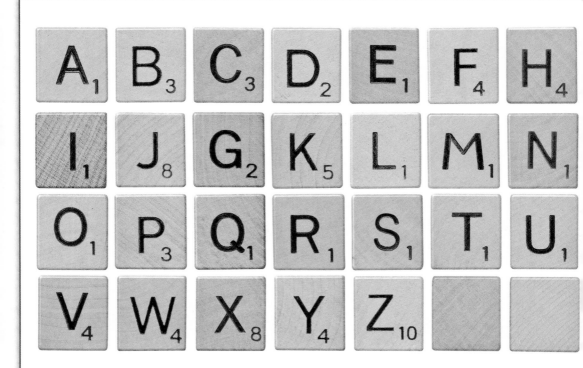

You win points in Scrabble by forming words with the tiles you are given. Math Scrabble works similarly, only the letters are replaced with numbers and symbols.

You can either make the game board and tiles on your own or you can adapt the board and pieces from an existing Scrabble game kit. If you adapt existing tiles, you will need to write the numbers on the backs of the tiles with permanent marker.

Depending on the grade of the classroom, you can include math concepts like exponents, square roots, and variables. The way the game is played is up to you! Teachers can help you determine the point values of each tile as well.

Once the board is set up, teachers can work together with your group to determine rules for the Math Scrabble games. Just like the regular word version of Scrabble, different tiles can be worth different points in this game.

Once you create the tiles, the object of the game relies mainly on you, the students, depending on age level, grade,

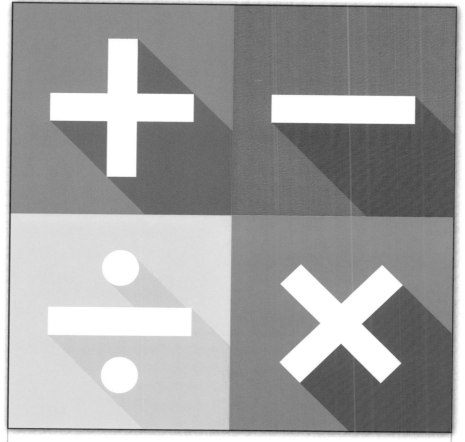

Addition, subtraction, division, or multiplication signs can be added to your Math Scrabble game. If you feel like you are ready for the challenge, go for it!

and ability. The game can be adding up prime numbers, matching odds and evens, or something that demonstrates that you know about numbers and equations. A more advanced approach would be using tiles that have symbols (=, <, >) to create true and false equations. Again, this all depends on the ability level of the makers involved. Makers can use these signs to add on to existing equations to make them true and also to earn more points.

For this makerspace project, the object of Math Scrabble will be forming equations. The rules are similar to the normal Scrabble game. You must have a set amount of tiles at all times while playing (normal Scrabble has seven at a time). Instead of forming words, however, equations will be formed.

Example: $2 \times 2 = 4$

In the above equation, you are allowed to add to the equation on both ends. That way, the original equation $2 \times 2 = 4$ can be turned into $22 \times 2 = 44$. Other rules, including the way the game is scored and when the game truly ends, can be determined by the teacher in charge of the makerspace.

The goal of this project is to have you learn about simple equations while creating a fun, interactive game board. This project uses simple arts and crafts building and design. Math Scrabble is an excellent makerspace project for those with little experience. The project is simple to do and will help you learn about equations.

This makerspace project is a good introduction for using makerspaces. Participants can be split into groups and given

ORDER OF OPERATIONS

One topic that can be covered in this makerspace project is order of operations. Students can create tiles with parentheses, exponents, and division signs in order to include order of operations. Order of operations tells you which operations to perform first in an equation. The common way of remembering order of operations is PEMDAS. This stands for "Parentheses, Exponents, Multiplication, Division, Addition, and Subtraction." Makers can demonstrate their knowledge of order of operations by following these steps while playing Math Scrabble. It is yet another way that the makerspace can be used to display a math concept.

their own responsibilities. In a group of three, one person can be in charge of making the tiles, one can come up with scoring rules, and the other can be in charge of making sure the math concepts are stressed during the project.

PROJECT 2: BUILDING KITES

Simple equations were covered in the Math Scrabble game. But that is only one makerspace project that students and teachers can work together on. While Math Scrabble covers the concept of simple equations, it does not cover other mathematical topics.

They may just seem like fun toys, but kites can also teach you a lot about shapes and other geometric concepts.

One such concept is geometry. The Math Scrabble game dealt with numbers and symbols, *not* shapes and angles. Luckily, there is a project that deals with triangles, right angles, parallelograms, and other geometric figures.

It is curious to note that the kite has its own specific meaning in terms of math. An object is a kite if it is a quadrilateral. A quadrilateral in geometry is a polygon

KITES AND ENGINEERING

While this makerspace project is about geometric figures, there is another concept that can be discussed: engineering. Engineering is a subject that focuses on the design, building, and use of structures, engines, and machines. Makerspace projects are a simple form of engineering as the projects involved all use some aspect of building and design.

An introduction to engineering can be useful with the kite makerspace project. Makers can learn which kite structures work best in different conditions, such as severe wind and other weather patterns. You can take an extra step from just constructing your kites. By testing them in real-life situations, you can figure out if a career in engineering is right for you!

with four sides and four corners. In geometry, a kite is any quadrilateral whose sides can be grouped into two pairs of equal-length sides that are next to one another.

Designing and building a kite is an interesting makerspace project. As you progress with the project, different math concepts can be introduced and explored. The shapes of the kite itself can be linked to different geometric shapes (triangles, squares, quadrilaterals, and so on). For this project, we will make a diamond-shaped kite.

This makerspace project is slightly more advanced than Math Scrabble. Gather materials first. These will be 2-ply plastic bags at least 2 feet (.6 meters) wide and 4 feet (1.23 meters) tall. Also purchase a flying line and two hard wood

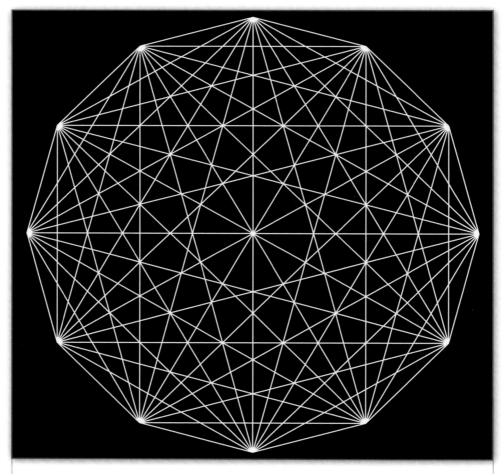

Making a kite is an effective makerspace project since it requires teamwork to make a kite that can fly as well as knowledge of various geometric ideas.

dowels about $^3/_{16}$ inch (5 millimeters) in diameter from a hobby shop. A roll of electrical tape rounds out the materials.

First, decide which shape of kite to make. The most common kind of kite has a diamond shape. To construct it, lay your plastic bag on the floor with the closed end on top. Mark two dots at the left edge of the kite, one at the top left hand corner and one 30 inches (76 centimeters) below it. The third dot should be 10 inches (25 centimeters) below the top left hand corner and 20 inches (50 centimeters) over. Next, connect the dots into lines using a pen and ruler. Cut along these lines. Open the bag to display a diamond shape, and attach the dowels vertically and horizontally with electrical tape. Tie the flying line at the spot where the wooden dowels intersect, leaving plenty of line to fly the kite. Attach a scrap of plastic for the tail and it is finished!

When making the kites, the makers may have a checklist with them that tests them on their knowledge of certain geometric terms. Examples of this include:

Are both pairs of opposite sides of the kite *parallel?*
Are both pairs of opposite sides of the kite *congruent?*
Are the diagonals of the kite *congruent?*
Are the diagonals of the kite *perpendicular?*

As you can see, these questions teach about different geometric concepts.

CHAPTER THREE

BASIC PROJECTS (PART 2)

The kite makerspace project and the Math Scrabble makerspace project are only two examples of makerspace projects you can create. What these first two makerspace projects have in common is that they do not require any complex materials. Game tiles and kite-making materials can all be found very easily. The next makerspace project is along those lines as well.

PROJECT 3: PAPER POLYHEDRA

This project is about the construction of paper polyhedra. Polyhedra are 3D models of polygons. They all contain flat faces and straight edges and can be folded like a cardboard box. This is a simple makerspace project that allows makers to experiment with creating shapes in various dimensions. The necessary materials are construction paper, tape, and scissors.

The participants in this makerspace project must choose what kind of polyhedra they wish to create. This makerspace project is very similar to the kite-building one. You must be able to identify which

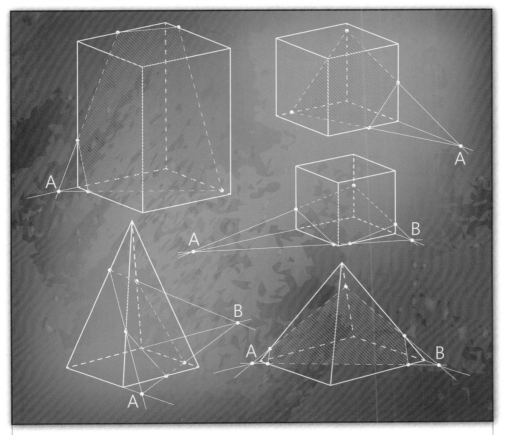

These are several examples of polyhedra you can make in the makerspace project in this chapter. Like the kite project, you will learn about angles and other geometric ideas.

polygons (triangles, rectangles, and so on) you are modeling your paper projects after. Assemble cardboard or poster paper and pens. Consult website resources to model your polyhedra after. Once your group decides which polyhedra to use, you can download the designs and get to work on your project.

Like the kite-building and Math Scrabble makerspace project, this project has arts and crafts elements involved. While you cut out and develop your own polyhedra, you are also learning about geometry. Makers can be tasked with proving they know about the shapes they are cutting and crafting. Then, once the paper polyhedra are complete, students can discuss what polygons they chose as well as why they chose them.

PROJECT 4: LEGO® SYMMETRY

This makerspace project uses a building tool that you should be very familiar with: Legos! Legos are classic building tools, and you may very likely have already been exposed to them. But Legos also can be used in makerspace projects to teach math. This project will be used to teach about symmetry, which is when an object is made up of exactly similar parts facing each other.

In groups of two or three, your task is to create a figure using Lego blocks. The teacher can decide how many lines of symmetry the object must have. The Lego structure can show one line of symmetry or several. However, it is important to note that you must be able to determine how many lines of symmetry there are. You may want to request a Lego building plate in order to construct your Lego figure.

After the figure is completed, you must show the lines of symmetry in your figure. Teachers can give you a piece of string that goes across your figure to display one example of symmetry

A Lego building plate is a helpful (but not required) component of this makerspace project. The project will help you learn about symmetry.

found in your figure. You can number off the lines of symmetry using index cards, and once you are done you can then prove and discuss the symmetry found in your Lego figures.

The construction of the polyhedra and the Lego symmetry project are two makerspace projects that are extensions of the Math Scrabble and kite-building makerspace projects. These

SYMMETRY IN THE REAL WORLD

Symmetry is a concept that has fascinated people for thousands of years. The idea is found everywhere in nature and also in art, architecture,

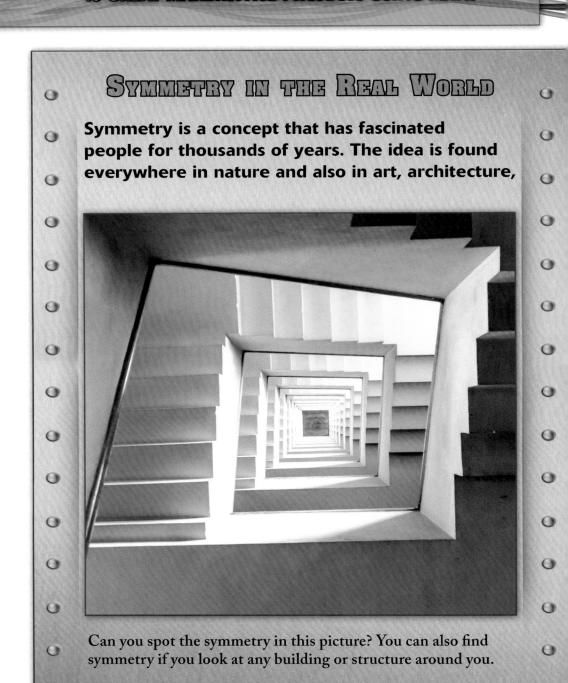

Can you spot the symmetry in this picture? You can also find symmetry if you look at any building or structure around you.

and design. Patterns in clothing as well as buildings all contain some aspect of symmetry. Go off on your own outside of the classroom to analyze symmetry in your everyday life; you will find it everywhere once you look for it. The Lego project is just one way to learn about symmetry. Patterns and shapes are all around you, and there's no limit to what you can learn about this topic both in and out of the classroom.

first four makerspace projects all share the idea of examining math concepts using very simple materials. These projects are very useful for classrooms that may not have the same tools and gadgets that would allow them to do more complex makerspace projects. They all use simple materials in order to teach you about geometric figures, equations, symmetry, and other math concepts. But there are even more topics and gadgets to be explored!

CHAPTER FOUR

MINECRAFT!

The first couple of makerspace projects have displayed how students and teachers can come together to build projects that help them understand concepts in algebra and geometry. But that is only the tip of the iceberg. There are many more makerspace projects that can help teach you about math concepts.

Not every classroom will have the same gadgets and tools as another. However, computers can be found in many classrooms. They can also be used for makerspace projects.

PROJECT 5: MAKERSPACE STRUCTURES

Throughout the projects already covered, teachers and makers have been tasked to create their own projects and their own worlds. While this is a key part of any makerspace project, there are some that use tools that are already set in place.

One of the biggest technologies that you can use when creating your own makerspaces is *Minecraft*.

Minecraft has become a huge phenomenon not only as a kid's game but also as a learning tool with various uses in the classroom.

Minecraft is a video game in which players can design and develop various buildings and construction using cubes in a 3D world. It's one of the most popular games for young children. Kids create huge, sprawling worlds and it helps them develop their creativity.

MINECRAFT: EDUCATION EDITION

Minecraft has become so popular with teachers that a version has been created solely for the classroom. *Minecraft: Education Edition* is a version of *Minecraft* that enables teachers and students to create and develop their very own makerspace projects. Created five years ago, *Minecraft: Education Edition* now reaches over a thousand schools, inspiring countless teachers and makers to develop their own projects. *Minecraft: Education Edition* lets students develop various skills, including coding, engineering, and various other STEM skills. It also, however, is extremely useful when developing projects that address math concepts. *Minecraft: Education Edition* is a valuable resource for teachers to use, both for developing makerspace projects as well as lesson plans.

Makerspaces are a good way for you not only to learn but also to foster creativity. *Minecraft* has become something much more than a fun game. The game also serves as a learning tool for young makers and has many uses for teachers and students when learning new math concepts in the classroom.

Many math concepts can be taught in the world of *Minecraft*. Whether you're tackling scale models, ratio and

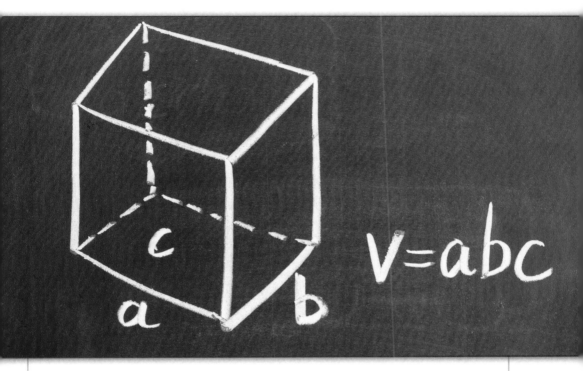

$$V=abc$$

Experimenting with *Minecraft* structures to learn about volume is one of the many uses the online game has in the classroom.

proportions, or area and perimeter, *Minecraft* is a useful tool in demonstrating these math concepts. The activity listed below deals with the concepts of area, perimeter, and volume.

While these concepts can be taught using worksheets and other materials, *Minecraft* is a good tool to use in order for you to learn about these concepts as well.

After each person has logged into his or her own *Minecraft* world, you can begin your makerspace project. Each maker must build four rectangular structures. These will all be used to figure out area, perimeter, and volume.

Finding out the area using *Minecraft* is easy. The formula for finding area is found by multiplying the length and width of the structure. For example, if you create a structure in *Minecraft* that is six blocks wide and three blocks long, you can use the formula to find the area by multiplying six and three.

Taking the same structure, you can now find the perimeter of a structure you have created in *Minecraft*. Once you know the formula for finding perimeter (adding the width and the length and then multiplying by two), you can demonstrate your knowledge of perimeter.

You can then use the structures in your *Minecraft* worlds to determine the volume of a certain structure in *Minecraft*. You can once again create projects in *Minecraft* in order to discover volume. Using the formula for finding volume (for *Minecraft* creations, length multiplied by width and height), you can discover the volume of your various *Minecraft* creations. To ensure understanding of concepts, you can create as many structures in *Minecraft* as you want, finding the volume, area, and perimeter for each!

PROJECT SIX: *MINECRAFT* EXTENSION TO BUILD A SCALE MODEL

Minecraft is useful for makerspace projects where you can create your own buildings and structures. You can use these structures to calculate area, perimeter, and volume. This was

Scale models are a useful tool in various professions, such as construction and architecture. They also have an important role in makerspaces.

seen in the makerspace project listed before. However, the design aspect of *Minecraft* can be used for further makerspace projects.

This makerspace project will have you build a scale model of an object. Because *Minecraft* is all about making buildings, you can choose to build scale models of a building of your choice. A scale model is a rough estimation of a certain thing (in this case a building) compared to the size of the actual building itself.

This makerspace project covers several math concepts. For one, you will be tasked with measuring your scale models and then comparing them with the actual size of the building you are modeling your projects after. You can display your measurements and compare them to the actual measurements of the buildings. This can be extended into a lesson on ratios and proportions. As your group designs your scale models, you can compare and contrast how your own designs measure up to the actual buildings.

Makers will be divided into groups of three or four and assigned different tasks in order to complete the makerspace project. Two can be in charge of designing the scale model on paper. The other one (or two) students can be in charge of using the scale model to design their structure using *Minecraft*. The students can match up their designs with the *Minecraft* structures.

But there is one extra step that can be taken in this makerspace project. Teachers can introduce woodworking into the project as a way of bringing your scale model and *Minecraft* designs to life. Again, like many other tools and gadgets, not every classroom will have access to woodworking tools. But woodworking tools are a good way of bringing your ideas to life.

Using both your written designs as well as your *Minecraft* creations, you can develop your own scale model buildings using woodworking equipment.

Scale Models in the Real World

A good way for teachers to stress the importance of scale models and designs is to discuss how they factor into the working world. Developing a model is an important step for many professions. For example, architects need a design model before they go to work on their building projects. Construction workers need design plans before they go to work on certain buildings. If a NASA scientist wanted to develop a satellite to orbit a planet, he or she would have to design a scale model of the satellite first and test it. Whether it's a scientist trying to explore the unknown or an architect trying to build a new apartment complex, scale models are useful tools. These scale models let these people know if their ideas can be put into action or if they need to be tinkered with instead.

Makerspace projects are a fantastic way for students to learn about life beyond the classroom. Experimenting and testing your ideas are common practices for many people in the working world.

IMPORTANT REMINDER

Woodworking tools, including handsaws and drills, can be extremely dangerous. Proceed with caution as you use these tools in order to construct your buildings. You will use these woodworking tools as an extension of your scale model designs, consulting their own measurements to cut the wood according to their models. Once this is done, you can compare your finished buildings to your original scale model designs and *Minecraft* designs.

Using woodworking tools is a great way for you to fully realize your own ideas. These tools also demonstrate various math concepts in projects such as scale models. Students designing their own buildings are drawing various geometric figures, such as rectangles and triangles, in order to create a finished product. Teachers can have students describe the relationship between these shapes as they continue with their scale model designs. The scale model makerspace project and the *Minecraft* project are both useful for this. You not only learn about measurement, area, volume, and perimeter, you also get to put these ideas into practice and develop projects that showcase your thinking and creativity as well.

CHAPTER FIVE

INTERMEDIATE PROJECTS

Carnival games are games of chance where players can test their luck in order to win a prize. However, tossing a ring onto a can or trying to pop a balloon with a dart is much more than just a game. Carnival games can be used to learn about probability. For this makerspace project, makers will be tasked with creating their own carnival games where those playing can win a prize.

PROJECT 7: PROBABILITY CARNIVAL

This project is unique in that it combines multiple projects (the games you create) to tie in with the overall theme of the carnival. One student group can be in charge of balloon darts or a can knock-down game. Another group can be in charge of a ring toss or a number wheel game. Once your group chooses your activity, you can then demonstrate what this makerspace project teaches: probability.

As makers come in with individual makerspace projects, you must also have rules that show your

A day out at a carnival can teach you a lot about probability. Many carnival games are simply games of chance.

knowledge of probability with your respective games. Take, for example, the number wheel game. A wheel should be numbered from one through ten. Then, using a spinner, you can choose how prizes are won. There are many ways in which you can do this. For instance, you can offer a specific prize for anyone whose spin lands on a specific number. However, this is also where probability comes into play. There is a four in ten chance of a person landing on a prime number. As players spin the number wheel, you can show the probability of landing on a specific number.

This can be modified further. You can color in parts of the wheel to change the probability. For example, on a wheel numbered from one to ten, color in some parts of the wheel red, some green, and the others blue. This way, the probability of coming up with a certain result changes.

For example, the three, six, and nine sections of the number wheel can be colored in blue. The probability of landing on a blue part of the number wheel is three out of ten. However, the probability of landing on a section of the number wheel that is both blue and an odd number is two out of ten. There are many ways in which you can change your

You can use different-color balloons to serve as different point values for your balloon dart game.

number wheels for the probability carnival. As long as your group shows knowledge of probability, whatever you decide to do with the number wheel is up to you.

Another game that can be set up is balloon darts. For this game, there will be a certain number of balloons each assigned with a point value. (Note: Depending on the age of the participants, sharp darts may be replaced with less dangerous ones.)

Let's say you use twenty-five balloons. Ten of these balloons will have a twenty-point value. Ten of the balloons will have a forty-point value. The remaining five will be worth one hundred points. Each player who plays the balloon dart game will have four throws. Prizes will be awarded based off the total amount of points after each player has had four throws.

You can then show your knowledge of probability by letting players know about their chances of winning certain prizes. There is a one in five chance of winning a one hundred-point prize. There is a one in ten chance of a forty-point prize and a one in ten chance of winning a twenty-point prize. Makers can also experiment with allowing multiple throws, but to begin, one throw will be given in order to win a prize.

The carnival probability makerspace project is unique in that it combines multiple games to make one project. However, all games will be used to show the probability of winning certain prizes. See which games work best, and you can experiment with various games to learn and master the concept.

THEORETICAL VS. EXPERIMENTAL PROBABILITY

The probability carnival makerspace project is a great way of teaching probability. However, there are two different kinds of probability that can be explored in the makerspace project. These are experimental probability and theoretical probability. It is easy to separate these two different types, however. The number wheel game is a good way to tell the difference between these two kinds of probabilities.

There are five odd and five even numbers on the number wheel. To find the experimental probability of spinning and landing on an even number, spin the wheel ten times. After ten times, record the number of times the wheel lands on an even number. If it lands on an even number seven times, the experimental probability is seven out of ten (or **70%**).

This is different from the theoretical probability. To put it simply, the theoretical probability is *what you expect* to happen in a certain event. Because there are five even numbers, the theoretical probability of the number wheel landing on an even number is five out of ten (50%). However, this is only what is expected to happen, *not* what actually happens. You can ask the game players about these different kinds of probabilities in their games.

PROJECT 8: BUILDING BRIDGES

The next makerspace project will use a tool that helps with any math makerspace project: the 3D printer. While it is good for you to brainstorm and design certain structures, 3D printers allow you to see these ideas and designs come to life.

3D printers have become an essential tool in many classrooms. They allow many projects to become fully realized, and they work off of student planning and design. 3D printers are extremely useful in STEM (science, technology, engineering, and mathematics) fields. They both enable and motivate classroom learning. These printers are now very affordable for classrooms.

This makerspace project will teach you the math behind building bridges. This is an interesting project, as it combines math with engineering and other sciences. How these different subjects intersect with one another can be discussed, but in this case the main focus will be on math.

This makerspace project has real-world connections as well. Teachers may stress the importance of bridges. All over the world, bridges, once strong and impressive structures, have deteriorated over time. A goal of this makerspace project is discovering what features can be added or modified to bridges to ensure they remain intact for as long as possible.

3D printers are a key component of this makerspace project. After you research different types of bridges and

golden gate - san francisco

coronado bridge - san diego

brooklyn bridge - new york

manhattan bridge - new york

These are just four examples of bridges throughout the world. Each one can be used as an example for this project.

their safety features, the project can begin. Bridges in real life must be able to support tons of weight, as thousands of people travel over them daily. Therefore, the aim of this makerspace project is for you to design a bridge that can hold the most weight.

While you work on your designs for your bridges, teachers may also ask you to predict why you think your bridge design will hold the most weight. As you complete your designs, you can measure the angles of your bridges and report back to your teacher on why you think those angles will make your bridges stronger or more effective to hold a certain amount of weight.

BRIDGES ALL OVER THE WORLD

The bridge project is a fun makerspace project, and it includes various bridge designs that are used all over the world. There are many different types of bridge designs. The arch bridge is one example. This bridge has structures called abutments at each end that are shaped as curved arches. Abutments support the lateral pressure of these bridges. The Sydney Harbour Bridge in Australia and the New River Gorge Bridge in West Virginia are both examples of arch bridges. A truss bridge is a bridge composed of a "truss," a structure that is made up of connected triangular units. San Francisco's Golden Gate Bridge is a prime example of a truss bridge. (Note that technically this bridge is both a suspension bridge and a truss bridge.)

Based on availability, you can design bridges using 3D modeling tools. Again, not every classroom will have this option, but the main thing to do is to make full use of the available 3D printers. You will be busy designing bridges as well as offering reasons behind why you believe your bridges will be able to hold the most weight. After the 3D printer prints out your design, the makerspace project concludes with the testing of the bridges that have been designed. This can be done by adding weights to the bridges to see how much weight the bridge can hold before it collapses.

You can be assigned to construct different kinds of bridges using the 3D modeling and/or the 3D printer. Half of the class can be tasked with making arch bridges, whereas the other half of the class can be in charge of constructing truss bridges. The results will be interesting to see. Will a truss bridge with a certain amount of angles hold more weight than an arch bridge with the same amount of angles?

This makerspace project allows you to learn the various math concepts found in the construction of bridges. It will also help you realize the importance of bridges in everyday life and how no bridge is exactly the same as the next.

CHAPTER SIX

ADVANCED PROJECTS

Makerspace projects range from the simple, like Math Scrabble, to the more complex, like 3D printers and bridge building. In this chapter, more advanced tools will be introduced that you can use with your own makerspace projects. One of those tools is robots. While robots also are useful for STEM projects, they can be used for math projects, as you'll see.

PROJECT 9: LEGO® MINDSTORMS: MADNESS WITH INTEGERS

Robotics is a huge advantage when creating makerspace projects. It is a great addition to the classroom and will make any math lesson all the more exciting.

Lego has a robot program called Lego Mindstorms that can be used for various math makerspace projects. For this project, the Lego Mindstorms robot will be used to help you add and subtract integers. Integers are numbers that can be displayed with no additional sign.

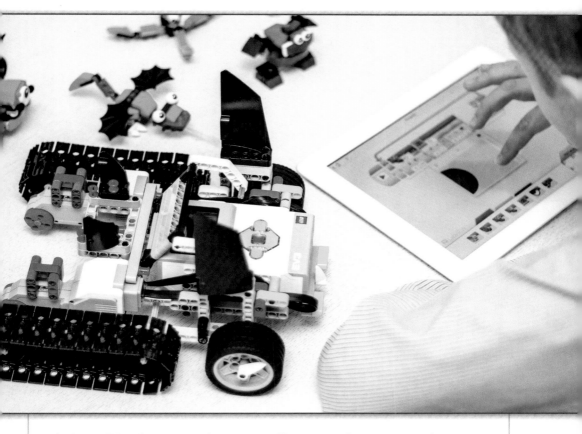

A Lego Mindstorms robot is an effective makerspace tool. Students and teachers can learn about their various uses in other projects as well.

Numbers like 274, 0, and –239 are all integers. Numbers like 14.35 and 7 ¼ are not integers.

This makerspace project is interesting, as the Lego Mindstorms robot will be used to perform different math functions. This project is unique in that you must learn how

47

to use the Lego Mindstorms robot itself before performing the project. You will need to build the robot itself. Teachers can provide a PowerPoint presentation detailing the steps to do this. The programs that you need in order to perform the project will already be loaded onto the robot.

Once the robot is constructed, you will be able to perform the project in groups of two. The only other thing required in this project is a number line. You will begin by placing the Lego Mindstorms robot on the number line at zero. Using touch sensors found on the robot, input values from the expression into it. The Lego Mindstorms then moves according to the values you have plugged into it.

The Lego Mindstorms robot's movements are based upon the integers in the expression. If the value is positive, the robot moves forward on the number line. If the value of the integer is negative, the robot moves backward. Because of this, students in this makerspace project will learn about integers.

You will use many expressions and examine the movement of the Lego Mindstorms robot. Based on the movement of the robot, you will be able to come up with certain rules about adding and subtracting integers. The next part of this makerspace project involves watching the robot's movement and then determining the integer expression the movement represents.

For example, you can program the Lego Mindstorms robot to move two spaces backward on the number line and then three spaces forward. You can then discuss the various

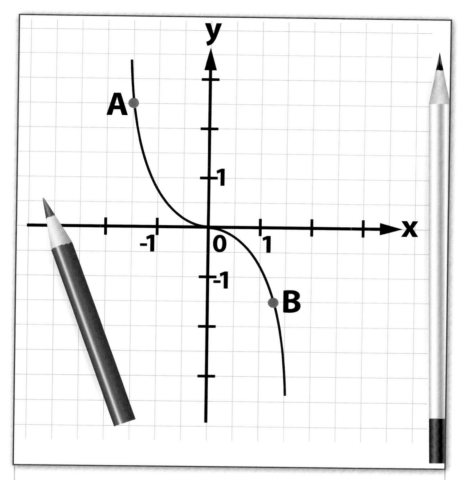

Graphing the Lego Mindstorms robot's movement is one step of this project that will help you learn about integers.

integer expressions this represents. Because the robot moved backward two spaces on the number line, that integer can be seen as –2. Moving three spaces forward is +3. Therefore, the integer expression can be seen either as 3 – 2 OR –2

+ 3. Either expression works, as it shows that the Lego Mindstorms robot's movement changed one space forward on the number line.

Take for example the integers 4 and 2. These are both positive integers. Plugging in these integers into the Lego Mindstorms robot will cause it to move from 0 on the number line to 6 on the number line. However, you can also change the value of one of these positive integers into a negative integer, and the robot's movement changes. Change the 2 to a –2. The Lego Mindstorms robot, instead of moving ahead six positive spaces on the number line, will instead do something different. It will move ahead four spaces but then move back two spaces because of the changed integer.

The final part of this makerspace project involves real-life problems that the Lego Mindstorms robot can model. The project will conclude by having you use real-life problems that show your knowledge of positive and negative integers.

You can devise your own word problems that the robot can demonstrate on the number line. There are many real-world word problems you can use. For example, let's say Student A has eight dollars. Student B asks to borrow four dollars. This word problem can be used for the robot. Simply plug in the first value (+8) and watch the robot's movement. Then, plug in the second value (–4) and then track the Lego Mindstorms robot's movement. You can repeat these types of problems and track the movement on the number line.

This is a more advanced makerspace project since the first part requires the assembly of the robot itself. However, once the Lego Mindstorms robots are set up, you can use them to display your knowledge of positive and negative integers. While this makerspace project is more complex than ones listed before, it is still a fun, engaging project that is worth exploring in the classroom.

PROJECT 10: LEGO® MINDSTORMS RACES

This final makerspace project is an extension of the previous makerspace project. In it, you programmed the Lego Mindstorms robot to move up and down a number line. However, in this makerspace project, you can program a robot to race against another one using math concepts.

The teacher can decide whether to use integers, equations, or another math concept to plug into the Lego Mindstorms robot. Each of you will be in control of one robot. You will be given a sheet where you will have to solve a problem and plug in the answer into the Lego Mindstorms robot.

This is where the teacher can get creative. He or she can program the robot so if you enter the incorrect answer, the Lego Mindstorms robot moves backward instead of forward. This will make you focus on your work instead of rushing to complete it. This final makerspace project is a great way for you to use robotics as a way to enrich your learning while having fun at the same time.

Along with races, students and teachers can also come together to have the Lego Mindstorms robot move through a maze. This involves advanced programming, but the main goal is to make sure you focus on the math work and enter the correct data into the Lego Mindstorms robot to make it move in a certain way. Again, it is up to the class to determine whether integers, equations, or another math concept is stressed as the robot moves through the maze. But with these two final makerspace projects, you will learn and discuss math concepts as demonstrated through the movement of the Lego Mindstorms robots.

Makerspace projects can tackle any math subject and use any material you want. There are limitless possibilities to what you can do! If there's a certain topic you wish to examine or a specific tool you wish to use, don't hesitate to experiment. Makerspace projects help various math concepts come to life and are fun ways for students to display and prove their learning.

Whether it is building a kite or using a Lego Mindstorms robot, makerspace projects are innovative ways for you to learn about various math concepts. A makerspace project is any project where you collaborate to learn about a certain topic. While 3D printers and robotic tools are nice, they aren't necessary for every project. There are no limits! Students and teachers can come together and create fun and innovative projects that allow students to both learn and create.

Other Makerspace Robots

Lego Mindstorms are just one type of robot that can be used for makerspace projects. Many other robots are available and can be used for math and STEM-related projects. Robot programs such as Cubelets, KIBO, and Dash and Dot can also be used to enhance any makerspace project. These

(continued on the next page)

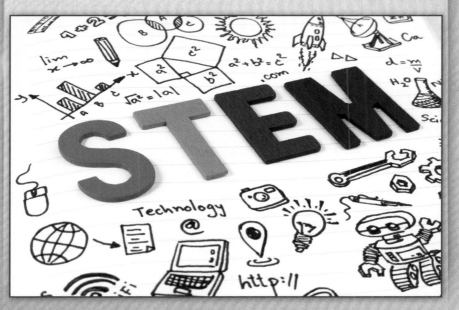

Lego Mindstorms robots are useful—and fun—tools for various science, math, and technology projects.

(continued from the previous page)

robot tools are a great addition to any math or STEM program. Teachers may decide to use these robots to show their students how math and science interact with one another. Math and science are very closely related both in and out of the classroom, and these various robotic tools can help show students this. These robotic tools are all available online and come with step-by-step instructions on how to build the robots and include various lessons and projects.

Makerspace projects can be as simple as a Scrabble game or can use complex tools like 3D printers and robots. Makerspaces are full of endless possibilities. A 3D printer or a laser cutter is a useful tool but it is not necessary for every makerspace project. Creating a project that stresses a math concept is a fun, interactive process. Whether you're discussing symmetry, geometry, scale models, or integers, there is a makerspace project that can help you not only learn but also engage in your creative side.

Makerspace projects are an amazing tool for any math classroom. These engaging projects are all around you, waiting to be explored and unlocked. Go out and create!

area The size of any surface.

congruent Exactly alike in shape and size.

engineering An area of science that deals with the design and construction of machines and structures.

integer Any number that can be written without any symbols (no decimals, fractions, and so on).

kite A four-sided shape that has two pairs of adjacent sides.

Minecraft A video game where players can design and build their own virtual worlds.

order of operations In math, the exact sequence in which equations must be solved.

parallel Being side by side and having the same distance.

perimeter The distance around a two-dimensional shape.

polyhedra Three-dimensional crafts that represent two-dimensional figures.

probability The chance that something may or may not happen.

quadrilateral A four-sided figure.

robotics Engineering that involves the use of robots.

scale model A copy of an object that is either smaller or larger than the object it is representing.

simple equation A statement (such as $2 \times 2 = 4$) that says that two things are equal.

STEM An acronym that is short for science, technology, engineering, and math.

symmetry Consisting of exactly alike parts that face one another.

volume The amount of space inside of a solid figure.

Canada Makes
1 Nicholas Street
Suite 100
Ottawa, ON K1N 7B7
Canada
(613) 238-8888
Website: http://canadamakes.ca
Canada Makes is a collection of academic and nonprofit
    groups dedicated toward advanced manufacturing in
    Canada. They use various tools such as 3D printers and
    3D imaging.

The Connectory
One Time Warner Center
New York, NY 10019-8016
(212) 484-8000
Website: http://theconnectory.org
The Connectory offers various STEM learning opportunities
    that lead young learners to explore and create.

MakerBot
One MetroTech Center
21st Floor
Brooklyn, NY 11201
(347) 334-6800
Website: https://www.makerbot.com
MakerBot offers affordable 3D technology and is one of the
    leading 3D design communities in the world.

Maker Ed
Maker Education Initiative
1001 42nd Street
Suite 230
Oakland, CA 94608
Website: http://makered.org
Maker Ed is a nonprofit organization that assists educators
    and students in creating worthwhile makerspace
    projects. They stress developing confidence and creativity
    through projects in technology, math, art, and science.

Makerspace Canada
412 Roncesvalles Avenue, Suite 217
Toronto, ON M6R 2N2
Canada
(888) 352-0899
Website: http://makerspacecanada.ca
Makerspace Canada offers kits, games, and toys for children
    of all ages to use for STEM/STEAM projects.

TechSoup
435 Brannan Street, Suite 100
San Francisco, CA 94107
(415) 633-9300
Website: http://www.techsoup.org
TechSoup is an organization that collects tech products and
    learning resources from various organizations and offers
    it to nonprofit groups.

The Tinkering Studio
Exploratorium
Pier 15
San Francisco, CA 94111
(415) 528–4444
Website: http://tinkering.exploratorium.edu
The Tinkering Studio is a section inside San Francisco's
Exploratorium Museum, set up as a makerspace for
visitors to create projects and be imaginative.

WEBSITES

Because of the changing nature of internet links, Rosen Publishing has developed an online list of websites related to the
subject of this book. This site is updated regularly. Please use
this link to access this list:

http://www.rosenlinks.com/UMFSP/math

Ceceri, Kathy. *Paper Inventions: Machines That Move, Drawings That Light Up, and Wearables and Structures You Can Cut, Fold, and Roll*. San Francisco, CA: Maker Media, 2015.

Daly, Lisa, and Miriam Beloglovsky. *Loose Parts: Inspiring Play in Young Children*. St. Paul, MN: Redleaf, 2014.

Dougherty, Dale. *Free to Make: How the Maker Movement Is Changing Our Schools, Our Jobs, and Our Minds*. Berkeley, CA: North Atlantic, 2016.

Felder, Richard M., and Rebecca Brent. *Teaching and Learning STEM: A Practical Guide*. San Francisco, CA: Jossey-Bass, 2016.

Gabrielson, Curt. *Tinkering*. San Francisco, CA: Maker Media, 2015.

Honey, Margaret, and David Kanter. *Design, Make, Play: Growing the Next Generation of STEM Innovators*. New York, NY: Routledge, 2013.

Lang, David, and Rebecca Demarest. *Zero to Maker: Learn (Just Enough) to Make (Just About) Anything*. San Francisco, CA: Maker Media, 2013.

Miller, John, and Chris Fornell Scott. *Unofficial Minecraft Lab for Kids: Family-Friendly Projects for Exploring and Teaching Math, Science, History, and Culture Through Creative Building*. Beverly, MA: Quarry, 2016.

Robinson, Ken, and Lou Aronica. *Creative Schools: The Grassroots Revolution That's Transforming Education*. New York, NY: Penguin, 2015.

Thomas, AnnMarie P. *Making Makers*. San Francisco, CA: Maker Media, 2014.

Bagley, Caitlin A. *Makerspaces: Top Trailblazing Projects.* Chicago, IL: Neal-Schuman, 2014.

Bardos, Laszlo C., and Samuel Carbaugh. *Amazing Math Projects You Can Build Yourself.* White River Junction, VT: Nomad, 2010.

Barnes, Mark, and Jennifer Gonzalez. *Hacking Education: 10 Quick Fixes for Every School.* Cleveland, OH: Times 10 Publications, 2015.

Burke, John. *Makerspaces: A Practical Guide for Librarians.* Lanham, MD: Rowman and Littlefield, 2014.

Dillon, Robert. *Redesigning Learning Spaces.* Newbury Park, CA: Corwin, 2016.

Doorley, Scott, and Scott Witthoft. *Make Space: How to Set the Stage for Creative Collaboration.* Hoboken, NJ: Wiley, 2012.

Fleming, Laura. *Worlds of Making: Best Practices for Establishing a Makerspace for Your School.* Newbury Park, CA: Corwin, 2015.

Graves, Colleen, and Aaron Graves. *The Big Book of Makerspace Projects: Inspiring Makers to Experiment, Create, and Learn.* New York, NY: McGraw Hill, 2016.

Hatch, Mark. *The Maker Movement Manifesto: Rules for Innovation in the New World of Crafters, Hackers, and Tinkerers.* New York, NY: McGraw Hill, 2013.

Kemp, Adam. *The Makerspace Workbench.* Sebastopol, CA: Maker Media, 2013.

Martin, Danielle, Alisha Panjwani, and Natalie Rusk. *Start Making!: A Guide to Engaging Young People in Maker Activities*. San Francisco, CA: Maker Media, 2016.

Peppler, Kylie A., Erica Halverson, and Yasmin B. Kafai. *Makeology*. New York: Routledge, 2016.

Roslund, Samantha, and Emily Puckett Rodgers. *Makerspaces*. Ann Arbor, MI: Cherry Lake, 2013.

Wilkinson, Karen, and Mike Petrich. *The Art of Tinkering: Meet 150 Makers Working at the Intersection of Art, Science & Technology*. San Francisco, CA: Weldon Owen, 2014.

Willingham, Theresa, and Jeroen DeBoer. *Makerspaces in Libraries*. Lanham, MD: Rowman and Littlefield, 2015.

ABOUT THE AUTHOR

Kevin Hall spent many years working as a teaching assistant. He has helped with many classroom makerspace projects that covered all subjects, including math and science. He also was involved with many math projects as a middle school student. He is excited to see how makerspace projects make a difference in the classroom and is curious as to how they'll develop in the future.

PHOTO CREDITS

Cover, p. 1 Hero Images/Getty Images; pp. 4–5, 53 Wittayayut/Shutterstock.com; pp. 7, 13, 22, 28, 37, 46 (background) Albert Masnovo/Shutterstock.com; pp. 8, 11 © iStockphoto.com/asiseeit; p. 10 David Gilder/Shutterstock.com; p. 14 Chones/Shutterstock.com; p. 15 © iStockphoto.com/JakeOlimb; p. 18 stable/Shutterstock.com; p. 20 elfinadesign/Shutterstock.com; p. 23 nuclear_lily/Shutterstock.com; p. 25 Ekaterina_Minaeva/Shutterstock.com; p. 26 BobEnasel/Shutterstock.com; p. 29 © iStockphoto.com/smontgom65; p. 31 Perfect Gui/Shutterstock.com; p. 33 Photology1971/Shutterstock.com; p. 38 Blend Images/Shutterstock.com; p. 39 PongMoji/Shutterstock.com; p. 43 photosmatic/Shutterstock.com; p. 47 AlesiaKan/Shutterstock.com; p. 49 Dahlia/Shutterstock.com; cover and interior page design elements © iStockphoto.com/Samarskaya (cover wires), © iStockphoto.com/klenger (interior wires), © iStockphoto.com/Steven van Soldt (metal plate), ©iStockphoto.com/Storman (background pp. 4–5).

Editor/Photo Researcher: Xina M. Uhl